FINGERPRINT
& DRAW
•ANIMALS & INSECTS•

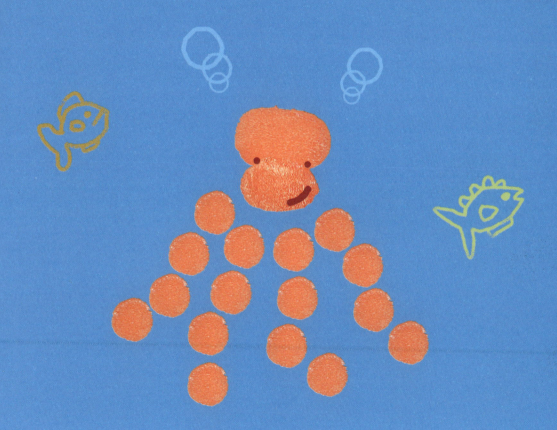

Walter Foster Jr.

MAÏTÉ BALART

TABLE OF CONTENTS

HERE ARE ALL THE ANIMALS AND INSECTS YOU WILL FIND IN THIS BOOK!

BUTTERFLY..........................4

GAZELLE & HIPPO 6

FLY & ANT 8

FISH & CRAB 10

CAMEL..............................12

SEA HORSE.........................14

SNAKE.............................16

CATERPILLAR & SNAIL.............18

CHAMELEON 20

OCTOPUS 22

SCORPION.........................24

CROCODILE........................26

SHRIMP 28

GIRAFFE 30

PEACOCK 32

OSTRICH 34

STARFISH 36

LION...............................38

BEE & BEEHIVE 40

GRASSHOPPER & BEETLE.........42

DRAGONFLY.......................44

DEER & LEAVES...................46

Quarto is the authority on a wide range of topics.
Quarto educates, entertains, and enriches the lives of our readers—
enthusiasts and lovers of hands-on living.
www.quartoknows.com

© 2017 Quarto Publishing Group USA Inc.
Published by Walter Foster Jr.,
an imprint of The Quarto Group
All rights reserved. Walter Foster Jr. is a registered trademark.

Translated by Juliet Lecouffe.

The original French editions were published as *Les animaux de la campagne* and *Jeux de mains*.
© 2014, Mila Éditions – 2ᵗᵉʳ rue des Chantiers, 75005 Paris

Thank you to Étoile.

6 Orchard Road, Suite 100
Lake Forest, CA 92630
quartoknows.com
Visit our blogs at quartoknows.com

TOOLS & MATERIALS

ALL YOU NEED IS YOUR HAND, PAINT, AND A PAINTBRUSH TO GET STARTED.

FOLLOW THE SIMPLE STEPS TO CREATE EACH CHARACTER. USE MARKERS OR CRAYONS TO COMPLETE EACH PICTURE. THEN DRAW A FUN SCENE AROUND THEM.

BUTTERFLY

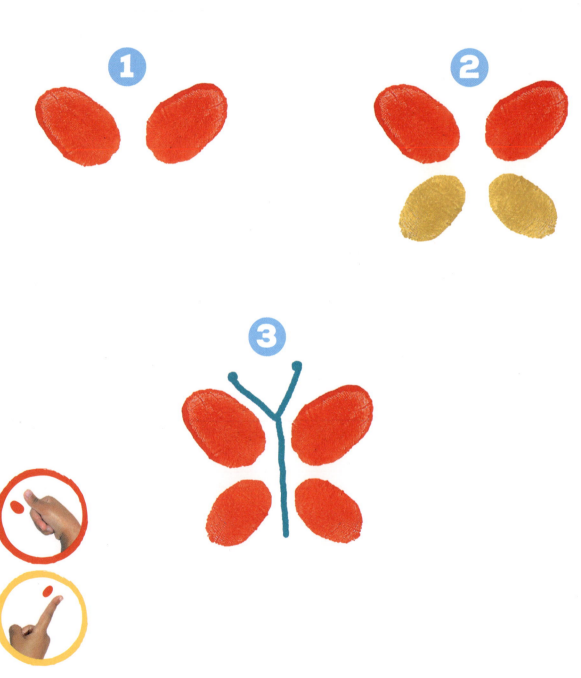

THE SCARLET BUTTERFLIES FLUTTER DAINTILY.

GAZELLE & HIPPO

GISELE, GABRIELLE, AND GINA THE GAZELLES PLAY WITH MAXIMUS THE HIPPOPOTAMUS.

FLY & ANT

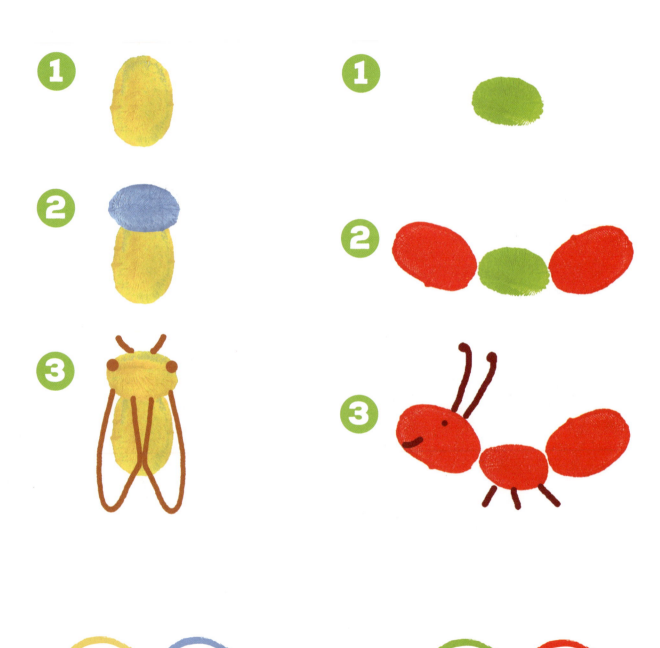

THE ANTS WORK TOGETHER HAPPILY WHILE THE FLIES BUZZ OVERHEAD.

FISH & CRAB

10

CLARENCE THE CRAB IS INVITED TO
THE BALL WITH THE FLIGHTY FISH.

CAMEL

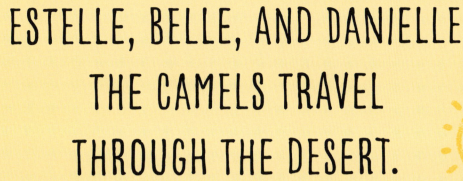

ESTELLE, BELLE, AND DANIELLE
THE CAMELS TRAVEL
THROUGH THE DESERT.

SEA HORSE

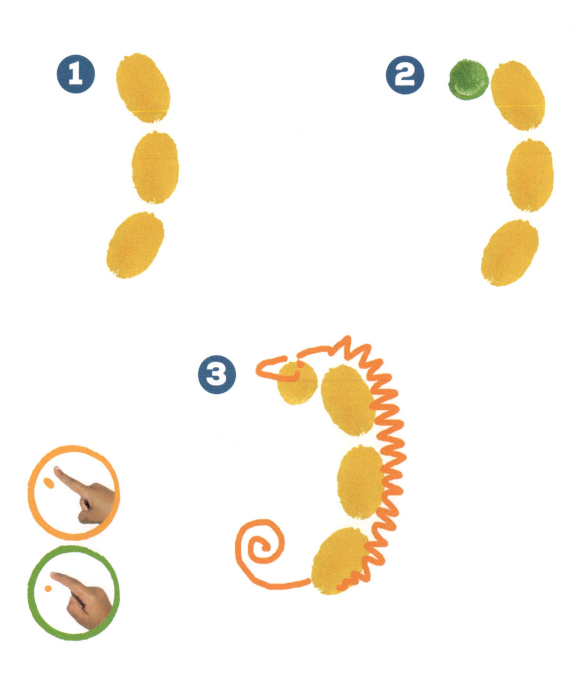

THE SEA HORSES SWIM THROUGH THE SEAWEED.

SNAKE

16

SYLVESTER AND SALLY THE SNAKES
SLITHER ALONG SLOWLY.

CATERPILLAR & SNAIL

CAMILLA THE CATERPILLAR DINES WITH GAIL THE SNAIL.

CHAMELEON

LEON THE CHAMELEON OFTEN CHANGES COLOR.

OCTOPUS

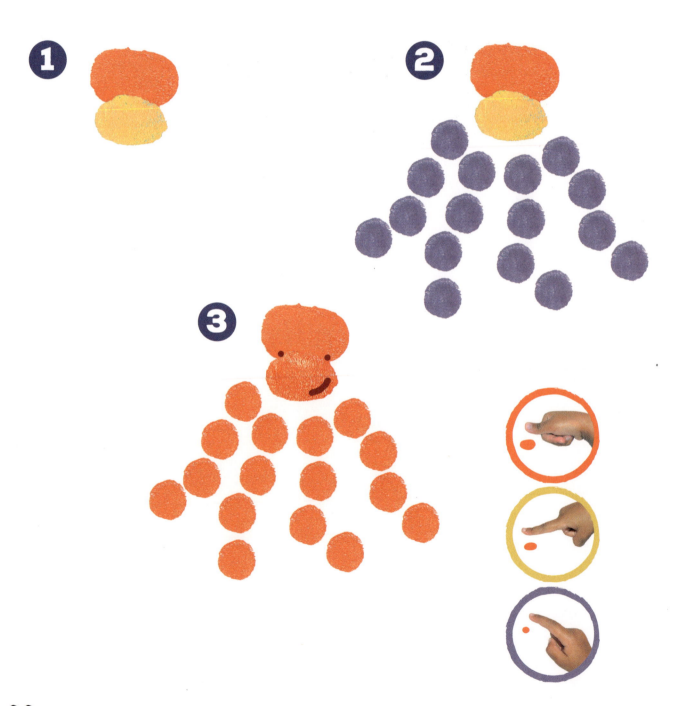

22

OWEN AND OLIVER THE OCTOPUSES PLAY IN A SHIPWRECK.

SCORPION

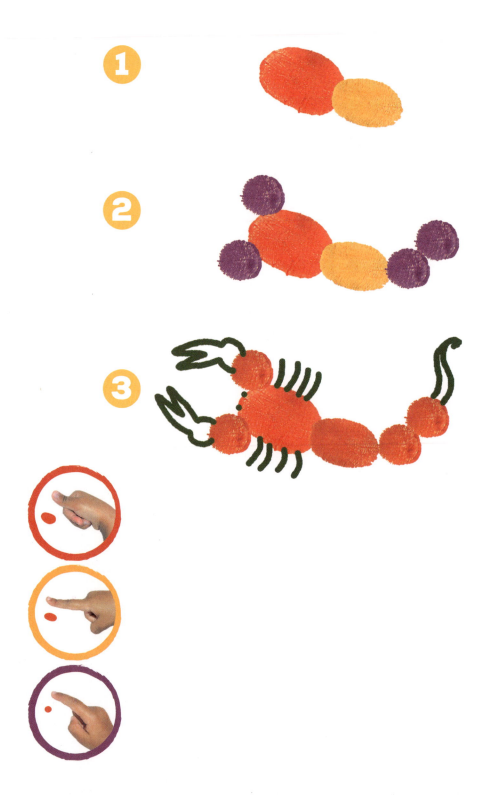

1

2

3

IN THE DESERT, THE SCORPIONS
SCURRY ABOUT IN THE SAND.

CROCODILE

1

2

3

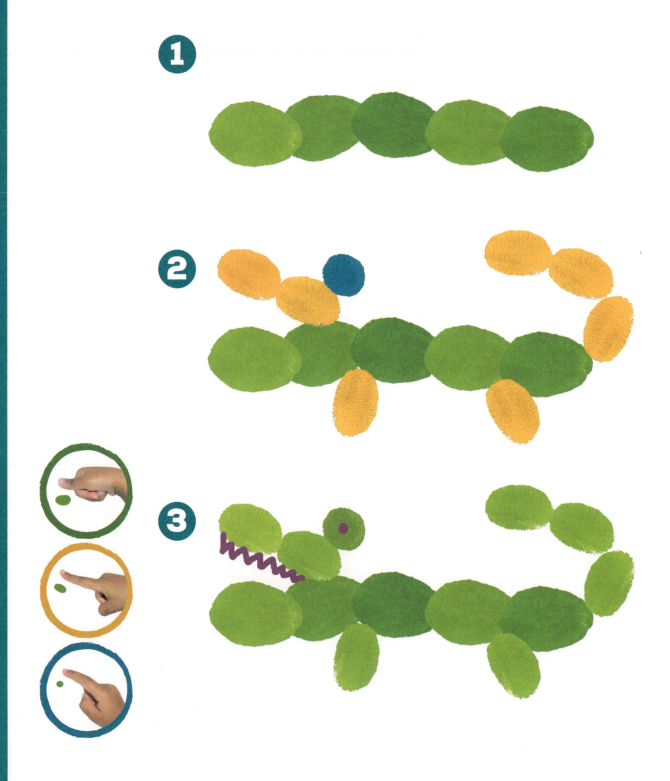

26

CHRIS THE CROCODILE LIVES
ON HIS OWN ISLAND.

SHRIMP

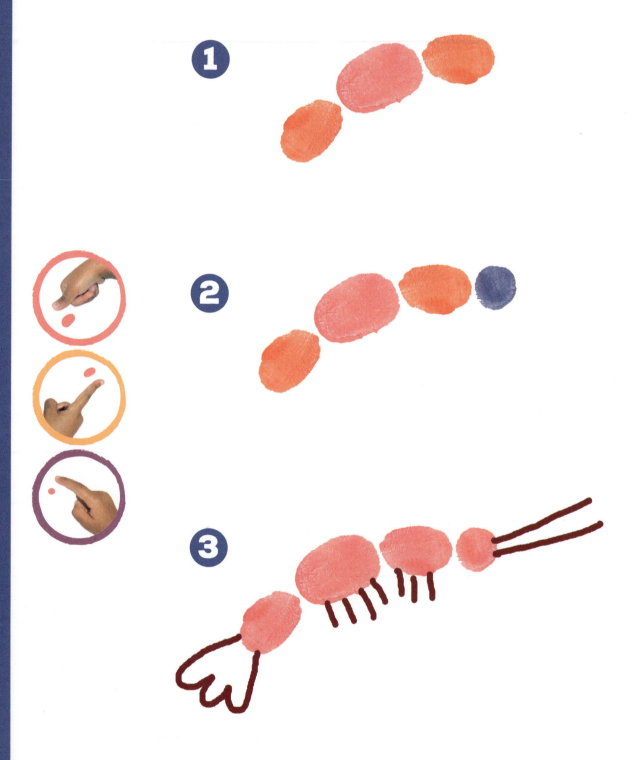

1

2

3

SUZIE, SALLY, AND SARAH THE SHRIMP
SWIM IN THE WAVES.

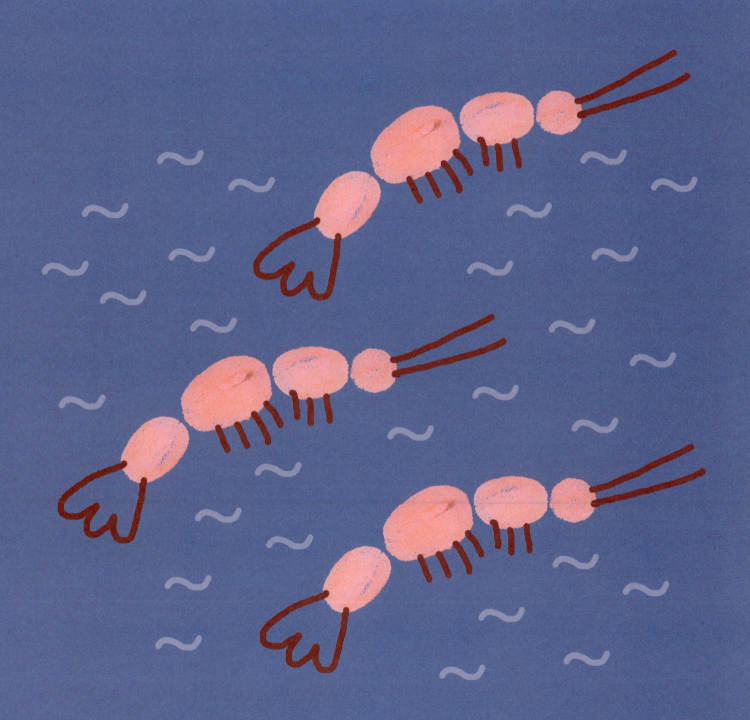

GIRAFFE

JACOB, JIM, AND JACK THE GIRAFFES
EAT LEAVES FROM THE TALL TREES.

PEACOCK

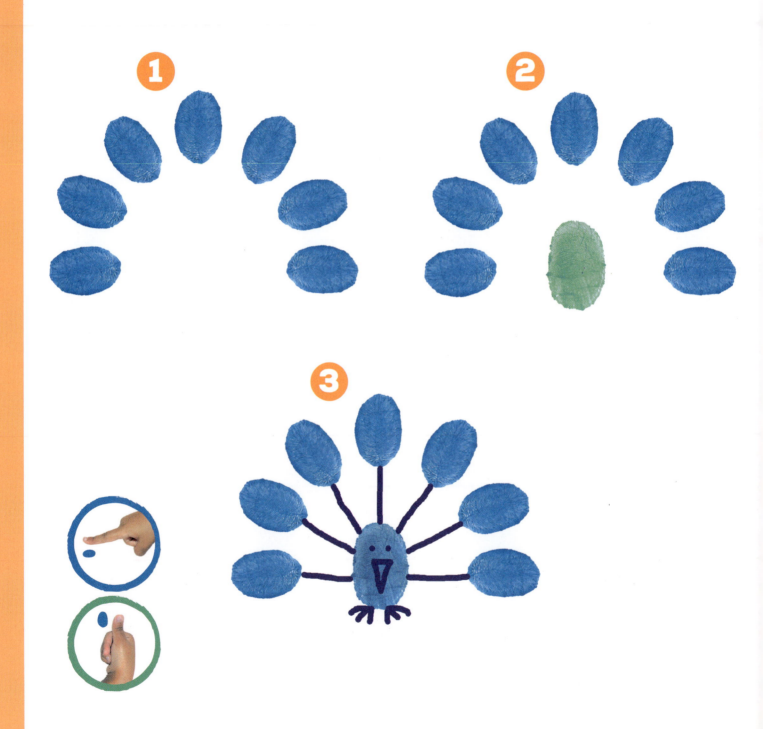

PETER AND PAUL THE PEACOCKS ALWAYS LOOK SPLENDID.

OSTRICH

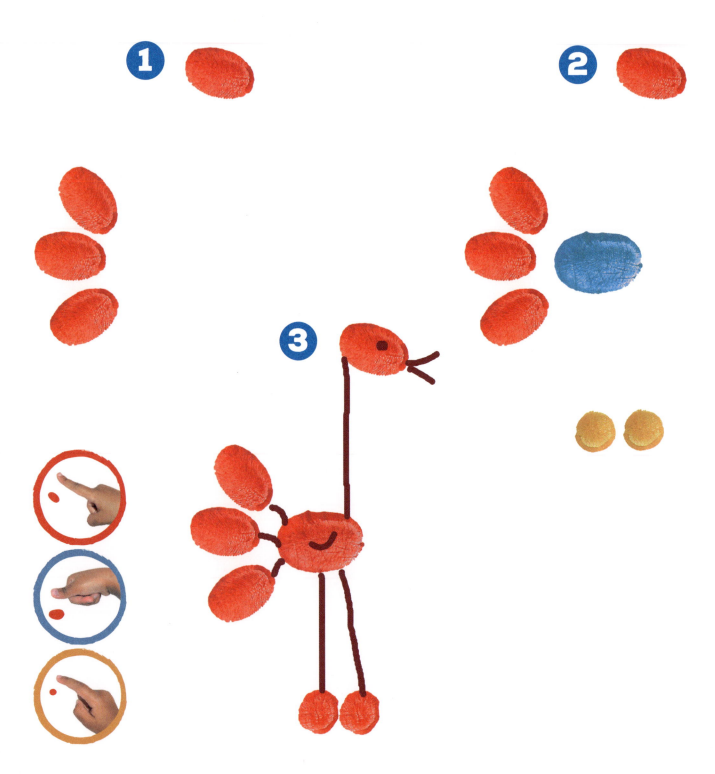

34

OLGA AND ORLA THE OSTRICHES
LOVE FANCY FEATHERS.

STARFISH

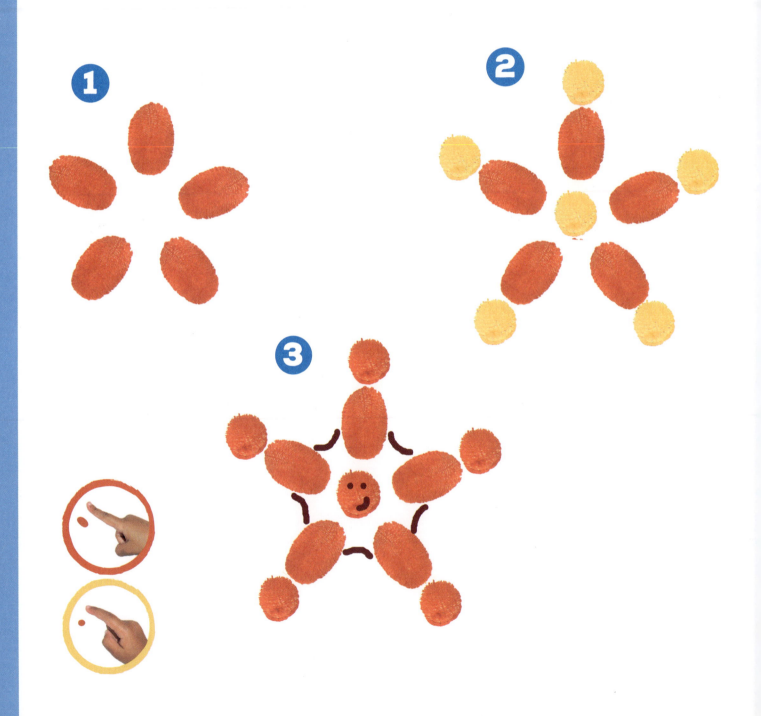

THE STARFISH ARE GOING ON A CRUISE.

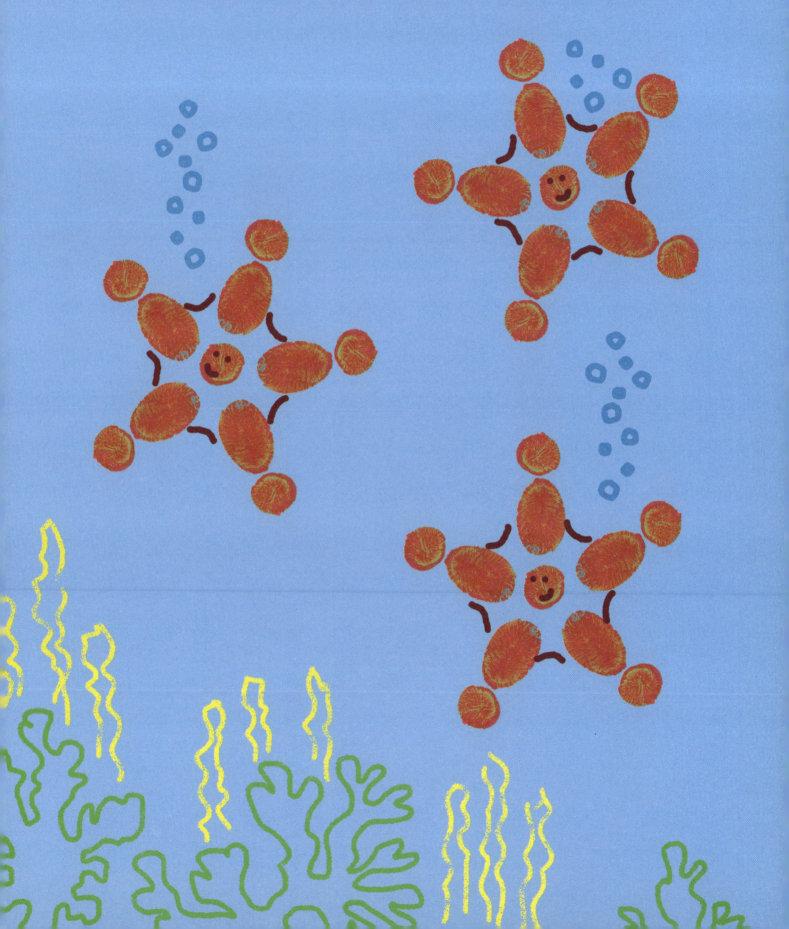

LION

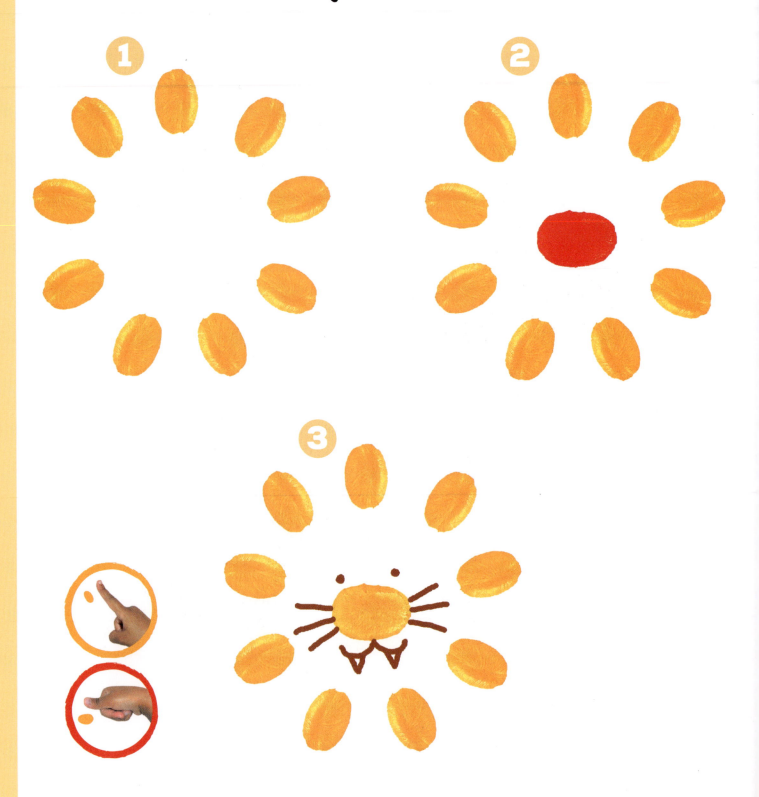

IN THE SAVANNA, SIMON THE LION
HIDES AMONG THE GRASS.

BEE & BEEHIVE

THE BEES LEAVE THE BEEHIVE AT DAWN.

GRASSHOPPER & BEETLE

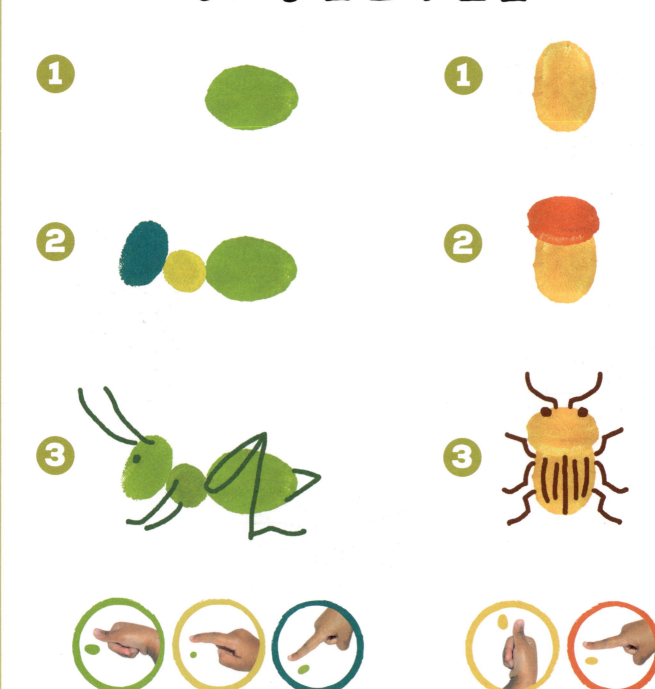

JIMMY THE GRASSHOPPER INVITES THE
BEETLES TO EAT POTATOES WITH HIM.

DRAGONFLY

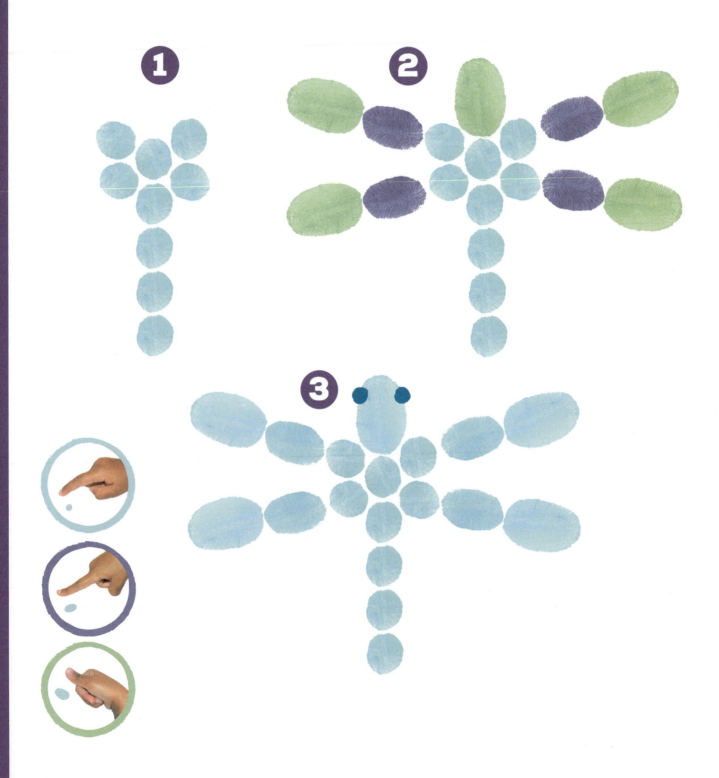

SKYE THE DRAGONFLY FLIES OVER THE POND AND THE WATERLILIES.

DEER & LEAVES

DAN AND DILLON THE DEER PEEK THROUGH THE LEAVES.

WHAT OTHER CHARACTERS CAN YOU MAKE WITH YOUR FINGERS?

CREATE A FUN SCENE WITH ALL OF THE CHARACTERS
YOU HAVE NOW LEARNED TO DRAW!

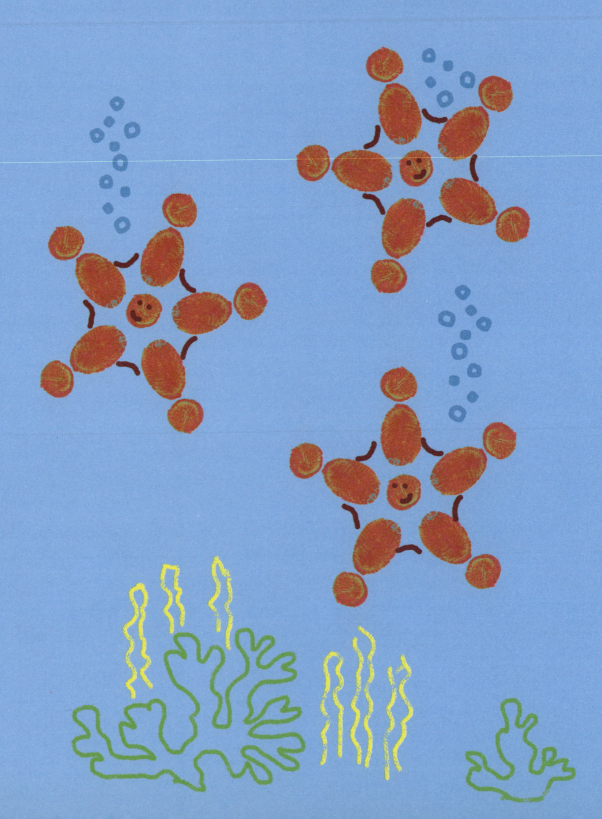